# BELOW
# THE SURFACE
# AND
# OTHER POEMS

OTHER WORKS BY SARAH LAWSON

*PROSE*
*A Fado For My Mother*
(Loxwood Stoneleigh)

*TRANSLATIONS*
*The Treasure of the City of Ladies*
by Christine de Pisan
(Penguin Classics)

*A Foothold in Florida*
by René de Laudonnière
(Antique Atlas Publications)

# BELOW
# THE SURFACE
# AND
# OTHER POEMS

## Sarah Lawson

To Carol
with love
and best wishes
from Sarah
8 July 1996

LOXWOOD STONELEIGH
BRISTOL

First published by Loxwood Stoneleigh in 1996

Designed and typeset by Falling Wall Press Ltd, Bristol
Printed and bound in Great Britain by Antony Rowe Ltd, Chippenham
Cover printed by Doveton Press Ltd, Bristol
Front cover photo by Sarah Lawson: *Stairway to Hypogeum, Malta*

*British Library Cataloguing-in-Publication Data*
A catalogue record for this book is available from the British Library.

ISBN 1 85135 027 6

## Acknowledgements

Some of these poems have appeared in the following journals and anthologies: *The Anglo-Netherlands Society Newsletter*, *Bananas*, *Critical Quarterly*, *English*, *The Friend*, *The Friends' Quarterly*, *The Honest Ulsterman*, *Lines Review*, *The London Review of Books*, *The New Statesman*, *Orbis*, *The Pen*, *PEN Broadsheet*, *Pick*, *Poesis*, *The Present Tense*, *Prospice*, *Quaker Monthly*, *Quarto*, *Radix*, *Reynard*, *Rialto*, *The Times Literary Supplement*, *The Urbane Gorilla*, *Weyfarers*; *New Writing and Writers 16* (John Calder, 1979), *New Poetry 6* (Arts Council, 1980), *Poetry Introduction 6* (Faber and Faber, 1985), *PEN New Poetry II* (1988), *Facing the World: An Anthology of Poetry for Humanists*, ed. Bet Cherrington (Pemberton Books, 1989), and *Outside the Chain of Hands* (Big Little Poem Books, 1994). The two sequences 'Dutch Interiors' and 'Down Where the Willow Is Washing Her Hair' have been published previously as pamphlets, by respectively Mid Northumberland Arts Group and Hearing Eye.

Loxwood Stoneleigh
St Andrew's House, 125 North Road, Bristol BS6 5AH, England

# Contents

## Letter with Enclosure

Dear friend, my camera
Has had another litter
And I send you
A keepsake sibling
To remind you of our summer
Later when the days shrink.
Keep this July light
Where you can touch it.
I send the low wall and the sundial,
The chestnut rich with leaves.
I send you that Tuesday moment
Caught, pressed flat,
Matt, four-by-six, to frame.

# Redecorating at the British Museum

The queen in the granite wig
Wears a plastic veil
Against the scattered showers
Of thick, pale rain – magic and indoors.

This rare Egyptian dyad
Of half as much again BC
As this is Anno D
Is tented for the week
As scaffolding rises like hosannas
To Amon-Re, tiers of planks,
Mondrian mixing with the monoliths
Of Luxor. Priests in white overalls
Oversee the esoteric rites
And wave their stubby wands against the walls.

The scribe with hieroglyphs
Down his apron to his feet
Squats taking notes,
Recording this holy week
When priests wrote white hieratic texts
Never to be Rosetta'ed off the wall.
The priestly whispers swish across the hall
In friezes of cryptic lemon writing
Up as far as the magic, sunless lighting.

## Burning Bicycle

Before the firemen come I peer into the house
Where fire is in control and out of control.
I have raised the alarm, but I can only
Tattle on the flames, gossip by phone
About them, instigate confrontations
From a place of careful safety.
Now through the front door oddly open
I watch a child's bike burn.
The flames are bike shaped;
They envelop every part like gentle packing
To protect the tyres and paintwork.
Bicycles are flammable, I generalise
For future reference. This pre-dawn awfulness
Will stay with me; I recognise this new possession,
A memory I do not much want
But must make room for somewhere.
Later in the coroner's court I bring out
My month-old picture for inspection.
It is ticked off a list, but I must take it home.

## The Monkey

Little monkey, my cousin, sits wisely
On a perch in a pet store cage.
Below her, children poke listlessly
At kittens, parrots, mice.
The monkey picks a thread from the bars
With thumb and forefinger,
Drops it exactly as I would,
Finding a stray thread on my bars.
Her delicate fingernails are purplish,
Perfect, curving on her fingertips.
Agile as youth, solemn as age,
She sits on her perch
With her feet informally against the bars
Like one in the front row
Before some entertainment.
My cousin has good manners,
Sits waiting politely, looks about
Without catching any eye.
She courteously hides her boredom,
Takes a casual interest
In the forms of life around her.
I want to strike up a conversation
And apologise for her being here.
I want to offer sympathy,
Give her my address, shake hands –
I want her to think well of me,
Distinguished little cousin of unknown age
Sitting politely like a guest
In her ugly cage.

## In Five Minutes

Now is the knowledge in the stomach
Of not performing just yet,
But in five minutes, in four-and-a-half,
I shall be observed
Moving these muscles, speaking,
Behaving in precisely this way.
They will say later
'What is it this reminds me of?
What vague thing
Is on the tip of the tongue in my mind?'
And it will be me
Unintentionally
Hiding in their memories
Like snow in a shady corner
Some thawing March.
Who knows where I shall be
When these harmless time bombs
Pop? Who knows exactly what
Will have dried in the corner,
What imperfect porous snow
They will notice
Some thawing March?

# An Evening of Flamenco Dancing

The clapping goes according to a science
I have not grasped, accompanied
By a castanetting with the feet.

Spotlights aimed straight at their crowns
Throw shadows down, dramatic.
Everything is red or black.
They pose, strike shapes,
Then hop into a home-made drum roll,
Heel and toe too fast to see.
The guitar men bending over their laps
Choose a few notes to furnish the stage.

When we finally clap in our amateur
Freelance way, it sounds all wrong:
Shapeless noise.
                    The dancers can also walk;
They come forward to take their bows
Putting off the dance like a pair of shoes.

# Bridgehead

(for Maria Wnuk)


She was the youngest, a useful fourth
For the after-curfew games of bridge.
All through the war spades and hearts were high,
Not to mention mortality and prices.

Her parents with their doubleton of wars
Filled the wall safe with salt and candles.
While opposing armies met
Exactly in their town beside the Wisla
They sat it out grimly taking tricks.

In another rubber of the war
The Stuka made a line of holes
Across the house her father built
As she dived through the doorway
One step ahead of the gunner
Following her home from a resistance errand.
The Stuka screams at her
At certain moments even now
When more than fifty years fend off
Her youth, when diamonds and clubs,
Sometimes bombers and morale, were low.

# For Elizabeth at the Bus Stop

(January 1990)


Do you remember how we met
On Walnut Street one night in centre city
Both waiting for the bus? (All these years
Have bleached the number down to nothing.)
As we were alone (Was it late?
Dark at least) we spoke.
Your friendly tone surprised me
Faintly. I can call up that old surprise
Formed of pleasure and relief.
Perhaps you knew somebody else
In my white camp.
Elizabeth, how fine it was
To chat on that bus that night back then!

Somehow you removed that wall
That skin shades make
Even among the well-disposed
In a country where colour carries
All that boring baggage.
We sat there in our early twenties,
And when I told you
I was a student, you beamed sincerely,
As though you were delighted,
On my side, absolutely happy
For my sake.
              Dear Elizabeth,
What generosity in the circumstances
Of the sixties when you grinned at me
And said, 'You've got what it takes!'
As if you really knew, you who'd met me
A moment before at Walnut and Twelfth.

16

I got off at Forty-third,
And Philadelphia hid us
Again from each other.
Elizabeth, bosom friend for half an hour,
It's you who had what it took.
I hope you've still got it. I think of you
Even now with more affection than you'd ever guess.

## Lines for Irina Ratushinskaya, Who Was Sentenced to Seven Years' Hard Labour for Writing Poetry

A poet explains good and evil
To people who already know which is which.
Even the authorities know what her poems mean.

Why are they so afraid?
They have a whole dictionary of ways to kill.
Why is this woman with her pen and paper
So powerful she makes the KGB have urgent meetings?
Her pen is dipped in something
That isn't supposed to exist.
They're trying to build a dam with bullets
And they're surprised when it doesn't work.

So the poems are dangerous, are they?
Punishable by hard labour and solitary cells?
So you're afraid of these poems
And this slim girl who wrote them
And threatens to write more?
She's got you covered with her pen,
And the safety catch is off!
Are the walls thick enough
To keep poems in?
Build the barbed wire higher
In case a poem flutters out!

The prison warders can't win;
Their characters wear down like chalk
Against the granite of their prisoners.
They are condemned to have their minds filled
With petty rules they have to make up.
('You're allowed only two sets of underwear,'
Whines the unspeakable Miss Podust,
Already far gone. 'We'll confiscate the rest.')
Their punishment is to be what they are.

They will never recover from it.
The prisoners have won, whatever happens.

## Cabo de Palos

Rollers come in like the wake
Of ships beyond the horizon
Out of sight under the blue edge
As I sit eating orange sections
On the balcony, January or not.
We mopped the tile floor yesterday –
Wet, it went porphyry-red;
It dried in shapes
Where the sunlight landed.

The offshore rocks balance on white saucers,
Some days nearly dinner plates.
The waves claim attention
Like the flames of a bonfire.
I watch them like a child
Eating popcorn at the movies,
A pile of orange peels on the plate beside me.
Progressing landward like the still but moving
Lightbulb news, these low-stepped terraces
Of bluegrass show last-minute white.

Always later, indoors from the wind,
I see across the glass-doored wall
The dark blue dado of the sea.
Late at night the sound keeps on,
And, inland bred, I think it's vaguely wasteful
And ought to be turned off.

# Going Up in the Eiffel Tower

Steel basketwork, like a cane seat
In three (at least) dimensions,
The Eiffel Tower is an old *clochard*
With a hollow leg
Where it stashes a little lift.

The cliché of it conceals
The wonder until the last minute
When the postcards fall away
And Monsieur Eiffel unveils his great design
Exerting no more square pressure on the earth
Than Monsieur Eiffel himself
Seated in a Second Empire chair.

On the way up to a still, stilted
Airplane meal in the tethered fuselage
We watch the Champ de Mars greenly sink
And Paris pop up like cardboard
In circle after circle of substitute horizons,
As though our motion upward
Makes ripples in the very Paris streets.

# *Camping Above Lake Komorze*

(Western Poland)


We have come out here
Where there is nothing
To get away from the lack of things.
Here we have a constant supply of pines,
Tall and well made, nothing shabby.
The sky holds every shade of red;
There's enough pink and orange
To go round without waiting
Or having to come back next week.
Everyone is at the head of a queue of one.

I disturb the perfect sunset
Rolled down from the far end of the lake
As a red carpet for the state visit of the night.
I swim across it, watching
The sun-slick break up, diluted into slats.

Crawling up the carpet now
(Warp and weft of evening
And northern late July)
I blink away the dripping sun
While behind me it ravels to the shore.
I'm telling my towel about the lake
When the drain beyond the trees
Empties the sky into tomorrow morning,
Where it's arranging another display of plenty.

# *Flanders, 1985*

Poppies for remembrance,
Poppies to forget,
Flanders poppies bleed
Along the roadside yet.

Battlefields are wheatfields
Where furrows once went deeper;
Cabbage carpets flank the Somme,
And they've long since rebuilt Ypres.

Now it's tourists and camping
Among the flowers and grain,
But there are graves at every crossroads;
Oh yes, the graves remain.

## Going Out to the Linhay*

(North Devon)

A new moon, a non-moon,
And when I switch off the electric day
And step outside, bits of sticky dark
Catch in my lashes, lodge like cinders
In the corners of my eyes.

The linhay perfectly matches the night,
Disappears against its background,
Then creeps into view
Turning into itself
As though in a red-lit darkroom tray.

The battery lantern throws a rod of light
That hits the linhay, lichen-dyed;
I tap along the walk, my white
Cane knocking the dark aside.

* Also spelled 'linney', a rural outbuilding in the West Country.

# Indiana Landscape

The land was good, the crops were full, but yet
From one year to the next we never had
Much landscape. Fence posts were the landscape
And then in summer, corn. You wondered where
The green came from on those coarse leaves; the grass
In August died from drought. Came the harvest,
And fences were the scenery again,
And sycamores. No hills, no mountains, not
A valley, gorge, ravine – no lakes, no sea.
Nothing to make you catch your breath.
Nothing people come with cameras for.
What we had instead was sky, and more
Than most. Our uninterrupted bowl
Gave us more variety than land
Could. Instead of mountains rearing up
Predictably, always in one place,
Our lightning struck down trees, our windstorms blew
Down houses. Kaleidoscopic landscape was
Our sky, making up for boredom
In the earth. At the Christmas end
Of years we had the blizzards, snowdrifts, ice –
At the patriotic end the dust
And heat, the slashing rain from livid skies
Irreparably shattered into little broken
Thunder pieces. With drama from the air
We had no need of drama in the earth.

## Cottage by the Sea

Our pine-wood cottage by the sea
Never intrudes;
You can hardly tell when you are inside
And when outside.
The windows let in the salt air
But there are vines on the porch
That shade you from the hottest sun.
In the evening we put on our heavy sweaters
And insist that the children wear shoes.
We walk with our arms folded tightly
In the fading light, with the sea wind
Living in our ears like the roar in a shell.
In the morning the room of white
And pine is sluiced with clear light,
Silvery and cool like the fish
In the net of the little motor launch.

Coffee on the porch again,
And a day of watching the sunlight.

# Robin and Pam on a Flying Visit

I'm giving them something I saw
In a restaurant with matching wine.
After their two-year stint
Before they go back again
I want to know
More than their hasty airletters said.
They borrowed somebody's car
And drove through the London rain to see us
On this week's arm-long list.
Tonight we have our own correspondents
From a place in the atlas open on the sofa.

He says down there
The monetary unit is the word for 'rain'.
'Rain' is the word for *hurray* and *best of luck*.
Outside our own less wonderful stuff
Spits and hisses at the window
Like a wet cat wanting in.
'They asked me once,' says Pam,
'What you call a river when there's water in it!'

Like thinking of what's in a vacuum instead of air,
We try to imagine and make sense
Of the wide dry wadi between here and where
They spend the rain like pounds and pence.

# North Sea Crossing

As dangerous as so much acid
This time of year,
The North Sea slugs it out with our keel
Somewhere below decks.
The boat's shadow lies on the sea
Like a dark bed of kelp
Growing up the starboard side.

On board this strange hotel,
All lobby and garage,
We sit like checked-out guests waiting for a taxi.
And our taxis wait for us,
Stowaways down where the waves
Slide their wedges through the sea.

Later we storm the beaches
In a highly pre-arranged attack,
Welcomed by the weary waves of customs men
Who know the outward voyage
Is the beginning of the voyage back.

# October on the Serpentine

Only one boat floats on the Serpentine today
In the chill breeze scattering yellow leaves
Along the edges where bare-legged women and men
Used to walk, throwing sticks for their dogs.
The lifeguards behind the lido ropes
No longer even play cards indoors;
They have nailed up a sign dismissing swimmers
And have gone home to rake leaves.
Our boat rocks on the pocked grey surface
Which reflects nothing, and when we stop rowing
Even the busy trees do not hear what we say,
For they are quarrelling among themselves.
Winter is rising in the west beyond the bridge
And the ducks talk of little else.

## Boat Race, 1980

Dragonflying fixedly,
The helicopter heli-hovers overhead,
Over the long April boats.

The eights skid their tiny seats
Over the Thames like skis
Disembodied from a skier.
Parallel, a schuss from Putney
To Mortlake, chased by
Unsporting engined craft.

The skiing waterboatmen
Leave no wake behind,
But the followers, facing
Those sweaty eyes discreetly,
Make waves that wet the feet
Of an intent photographer,
Make children hop like dancing cowboys
Shot at by the baddies
As the wash waves in.

Out of sight, they leave us
With the empty river,
The wakes drying up to ripples,
Changing their story to deny
Boats ever passed.
Only we on the bank
Can corroborate the oars
And little jockey coxes.

We go back aboard the bridge
To catch the landlubbing bus,
The Oxbridge boats reaching the flags
In Mortlake up the river
As we cross the street.

# DUTCH INTERIORS

# *View of Landscape: a Celebration*

Only Holland looks not merely washed but ironed;
The pressed brown corduroy of March
Brightens into green by May.

The zig-zag dikes go mole running
Past white Maltese crosses
Primed to put the wind to work.

Always at half-swords with the sea,
The Dutch steal a whole new province from the waves;
Their generals are engineers
Filching land out from under the enemy.

It's not like other countries,
This land the Dutch invented.

Too pretty to be lived in, the houses
Are scrubbed down by the light
Rolling in like weather off the sea.
Trapezoidal roofs the shade of flowerpots
Make every house a House of Orange.

## *Dutch Interiors*

The cobbles winding like a cowpath
Toward the market square
Are a dike-top doing double duty
As a street and a corridor
Past works of art. At night
The Dutch interiors hang behind the glass.
New Vermeers and Steens: card-players lean
On tables topped with fringe-hemmed ruglets;
Overhead a bell clangs quiet light.
Every street is lined with lit-up dioramas
For passers-by to share,
As though the street has been impoldered
Into living rooms. Behind the proscenium hedge
Growing on the window sills
The family is a display team of domestic life.
The wind in our hair,
We pass along the windows
Like guests at a deaf-and-dumb houseparty
Welcomed but unacknowledged by the hosts.

# Windy Morning on Schouwen-Duiveland

The wind is testing the trees this morning –
It sorts through the leaves
And throws out the loose ones.

The mountain ash
Is a wedding guest
Flinging confetti everywhere.

The towels lie under the clothesline,
Tossed off like a dancer's skirts
As the tempo quickens.

Still on the line,
Frantic shirts backstroke in place,
About to drown in a weir of wind.

## The Beach at Renesse

The long stairway over the dunes
Is a stile for giants.
I count the fifty-eight steps
On the landward side
As we creep up it
Carrying our seats and lunch,
Our swimming suits and caps.

Then we sit by the sea
In the chairs we have brought
Where the edge of the water
Curls into white lace.

Behind us the stairs carry bathers away
On a high wooden wave
Over the dunes green with long-rooted plants.
They are little bright figures,
Quattrocento on a Jacob's ladder
Up to a fresco sky.

Closer bathers stand in the sea
Waist-deep or less
Looking for a dime they've dropped.
They watch those stringy toadstools
Resting like spit in the water.

In the low shadow-throwing sun the beached jellyfish
Are smooth like rounded, dying ice cubes
Left in the bottom of the glass.
The blue ones that sting,
Indelible splotches from a poison pen,
Lie dead and harmless, little globules
Of what makes the girls shriek,
Shrill and squeamish in bikinis.

## Westerschouwen Light

By day the lighthouse is a barber's pole
Where the sharp surf shaves the dunes.
In the dark it doles out light, one radius at a time,
Wasting half of it on the land.

This cop on his beat
Makes the thieves duck
Twelve times a minute.

Westerschouwen Light,
Every time I catch its eye
It looks away.

# Hans and Anneke's Lakeland Terriers

*'Weet je niet? Weet je niet?'*
Say the paws of the dogs all day on the floor.
Their frilly, furry pantalettes prance
To staccato tap dance cleats
(*'Weet je niet? Weet je niet?'*)
Across the hardwood floorboards.

In the tired evenings the terriers lie
By the foot of the floor lamp
Like a pair of little brindled bolsters
Tossed down from the corners of the sofa.

# Messages from the Harbour

The deserted harbour is crowded with noise.
The boats in their off-hours fill the air
With derisive messages for the inland towns.
The wind loses them along the way, of course,
Like careless boys made to bear reports
And dropping them behind the barn,
Among the trees.
            The ironic ropes
Slap the hollow metal masts and mimic cowbells
To taunt the leeward inland folk.
A rush of hemp applause claps quickly
On other masts. The yachts all celebrate each other,
Exchanging little bows.
                Some spirit of the yacht
Wants out. The sails are bound down
And four ropes hold each boat
Like a bull being taken to the fair.
The harbour is a riot of tin cups
Banged against the bars.
'Out! Out!' chant the maddened cables on the masts.
But clamour and riot however much they like,
The message does not carry far beyond the dike.

## *The Harbour in February*

The harbour still rattles like the height of summer,
Now when the harbour basin's nearly walkable.
Like slim horses nervous in their stalls,
The yachts shy a little on their tethers
And keep some real water to be restless in.
The next week, though, is quiet with ice,
And the over-wintering boats are caught solid,
Motionless where they fidgeted in their narrow moats.

# Ice Skating in Brouwershaven

Over the formal white-gloved trees
The windmill pokes its clockwork rabbit ears
Just too far away to hear the skaters' oom-pa.
They flooded the old playground,
Inviting Jack Frost to run through it.
He came one night and hung around the place
Until half the town had red noses
From skimming counter-clockwise
Under the dim winter sun,
Dark figures on their annual slick sharp shoes.

Van Dam clears the frozen sawdust
Off the rink, letting the motored bottle brush
Pull him along like a sleepy water-skier.
Behind him like gulls in a tractor's wake
Little boys pick over the new ice,
Dark in brush-wide swathes.

Beyond the range of toy Alps at the edges of the rink
The hot chocolate van is mobbed by stocking caps
All wagging their tails. Flat-footed wallflowers,
Transmontane, watch the others dance;
Still on the far side of the harbour
The uninvited mill strains for a polka phrase.

# *Breakfast in the Train Station at Goes*

In the early morning fog
Everything looks unscrubbed.
The bus lights cast grey megaphones in front,
Shouting in mime that they're on their way.
The fragile bicycles are all fog
Between the white light and the red.

As I drink my coffee by the window,
In from the doorstep dark comes the day
With a huge bouquet of purple iris
Filling the sky. When I leave
The flowers have faded to lilac
And the day is rolling up its sleeves.

## On the Oude Rijn

Grebes nesting under the waterfall of willow
Watch our boat from behind their suburban curtains.
We chug on past the rugs of woven water-lily leaves
Set out on the river like saucers in the sun.

Down beyond the sluice we turn
To cruise back through the afternoon.
We tie a knot in the wake we tow,
Like the corner of a handkerchief for remembrance.
The loop unravels as we spurt away
And sinks into the green June water,
Down to where all the old wakes lie.

## Carrots

An extra roof
Lies among the farm buildings,
Orange and pitched like the others,
But covering only the farmyard grass.
It is October now
When the tractors scuff their dirty boots
Down all the country roads,
And the waggons haul in sugar beet
And carrots, orange as tile,
Heaped among the barns and sheds.

# *Windmill*

The wind breathes on these sails,
Feeding the teeth of one wheel
With those of another.

Creaking like a canvas-loaded clipper,
The factory and the machine are one;
The building works as hard as anybody else.

Now the grindstones digest the grain,
Driven by generations of cogs
Forwarding messages from the wind.

## Spring in Friesland

You give me your memories
In the ribbons and wrappings
Of a birthday-festive farmhouse.
I walk through your youth,
Admiring everything,
Like a visitor on a day
When the public's not admitted.

The tulips on the windowsill
Bend graceful goosenecks toward us,
Straining to hear
What makes us laugh together so.

## Thinking of Captain van Swearingen in the Beemster

They made the water lie down
And play dead.
Now the houses step in unison
Over their moatlings
On the way to the street.

I come to the Beemster
Thinking of the old captain,
A distant forebear, who sailed here
Until they drained his seaway
To make more of North Holland.
I look at the sky, which even the Dutch
Can't control. He would recognise that
And the clouds' moving, changing mountain ranges.

All these houses lie on the old sea bottom,
The church spire showing like a periscope
Above the surface of the captain's sea.

## Old Masters at the Rijksmuseum

They have preserved just the most transient things in the house;
The strum of the lute, even the fish still wet from the pump,
And the apple core before the maid picked it up.
The checkerboard floor converges on the past.
They've painted the conversation almost overheard
Through the gauze of three hundred years,
The music-master's advice nearly caught,
The churchwarden's tuft of smoke,
The hand of cards one candled night.

Now you cannot find their graves,
But they still laugh; their lives go on
Against these hessian walls,
Merriment for these five lifetimes laid end to end.

# The Wedding Guest

(for Jack Finch)


We didn't know at first whose guest he was
When he danced and then told jokes and made us roar
With laughter. Some of us asked each other, 'Four
Strangers came from Gallilee – because
Of Simon is it? Fishermen he knows?'
Then somebody said, 'You must know *him*! The best
Mimic you ever saw! He'll be the guest
Of both the bride and groom. You see, he owes
That fellow – the groom owes him a lot. I think
He introduced them.' When the wine ran out
Some started to leave. They'd had too much to drink
In any case. Then something happened – doubt
It if you must. That fellow – that Nazarene –
Made wine from water! Think, man! What can it mean?

# The Harbour

The harbour is a jackstraw jumble of masts
As complicated as a jigsaw picture.
A painter sits at her easel, another dot
Of colour in a red jacket,
Making another harbour
(Where brushless painters dangle in the water),
Compressing the furled sails still more
To fit on a scrap of canvas.
She paints a likeness of an unpainted hull;
She records the light on the harbour wall
As meticulously as a court recorder
Taking down the stammer of a witness.
Soon the portable harbour will hang
On a city wall where the pigment light
Will always dapple the harbour moss
And the noise in the street
Will sound like muffled gulls.

## Mexico City College

The arcade is stucco pink in the morning sun
And puddles lie on the tile patio
From last night's rain.
We sit with our textbooks and coffee
Talking frivolously, for it is morning.
At the next table,
A blind man and his dog –
A benevolent wolf who looks smart enough
To take a degree herself.
The cool rain-survived air here
Breathes itself without being asked.

Out in front on the highway
The old bus heaves up the hill
On its way to Toluca – the *Flecha Roja*
Full of live chickens and blankets for the market.

# The Footbridge

After dinner evening comes
Swirling its red drink
In a darkening glass.
The lawn and trees all seek
A median green.
Even mist from the lake rises green;
Only the footbridge is white.
It is still white when all the outlines
Around it have faded together.
Only the bridge in the twilight:
Leading from vagueness to vagueness,
From fallen leaves to fallen leaves.
Luminous white, spanning nothing,
By its presence an invitation.

## Pond in August

August willows like green Degas dancers' skirts
Trail in the army-green water
Linty with old feathers and early yellow leaves.
Ripples marcel across the pond
Ricocheting the changing, undecided light
Undersided to the plane tree leaves and back.
The plane inclines over the edge,
About to dive out racing flat.
Ducks clack gobbling castanets
To entertain some passing insects.
(They have no flamenco-flair in spite of
Daily practice; their forte is barcarole.)
On the island while
A duck tucks its shirttail in,
Some geese walk like monocled tropical diplomats
In white, harshly discussing alliances and pacts.

## Core Samples

I don't know where they come from.
Things get caught in the bits,
They come up on Archimedes' elevator
Or in this long hollow straw.
Scraps of affinities,
Fragments of inclinations,
Particles of aversion –
You can see them laid out
On this clean tarpaulin.
We can only guess where they fit in
With the rest of the stratum.
You may have this specimen, if you wish.
Not at all, not at all.
Some are denser, some lighter
Than others. They are like
Children's blocks;
You can build models with them.
I cannot think they are very valuable
In themselves. Take this one, too,
To go with the other.
They are only core samples, trinkets;
I don't suppose they tell us much.
Have this reddish one,
But careful of the edges.
They give an idea, I suppose,
Some sort of idea.
You are welcome to any of them,
Except for a few I have put aside.

## A Friend from Home

Even if I lived on Mars for years
And had good friends and liked my work
And learned to eat the food,
Any other Earth person would look
Like a blood relation to me.
This human, who might come
From any room of our common home,
Would speak with vocal cords
In the human way, would know first hand
About ears and eyebrows.
We would fall into each other's arms
In front of the startled Martians.
Any news of home would be of interest.
We would have our little private jokes
About the Pacific Ocean or oxygen.
If we didn't share a language
We would gesture and draw pictures,
The Martians looking over our shoulders
And shrugging to each other. I would ask
About trees. We would draw leaves and seeds
And shout with recognition.
We would draw birds' nests in the trees
And slap each other on the back.
Our Martian friends would sigh
And give each other looks and say
'These Earth people when they get together –
They always act this way.'

# Hamlet

This actor is no more Danish
Than I am; no more murderer or prince
Than I. Chances are
He's never seen a ghost.

Elsinore is a stage with sets
And curtains. The wardrobe mistress
Worked half the night
On Gertrude's third-act gown
To get it right.

The gravediggers dig a trapdoor
Halfway down to where the props are kept.

The fights need late rehearsals;
Hamlet and Laertes relax
At the pub next door before they catch
Their several tube trains home.

The state of Denmark's all a prop.
The only thing that's real tonight
Is Yorick's skull.
Human bone that grew and died,
It once held someone's brain.
Ignorant of Equity, the old owner never knew
He'd end up playing Yorick,
A role still more mature than Lear.
Death does his cameo walk-on here.

## Poet at School

Not lost, though often asked,
As I wander through this school
Just looking, watching, peering into rooms.
Maps and blackboards whisper messages
As I pass. This is where
A thousand people are all day.
Anyone merely strolling,
Merely watching and sensing,
Must be lost.

But it is all explained
Later in the staff room in lowered voices:
The tame arranger of words brought in
To coax native tricks of vision
From the thousand.

## Coming in Late

Coming in late I wake up the elevator
With a jab of my forefinger in its ribs.
It comes creaking and swearing
Like the porter in *Macbeth*
And yawns in my face
With exaggerated drawling politeness.
I think tinker-tailor-soldier-sailor
On its big clown buttons
And ride like a little Jonah
To a sixth-floor Nineveh.

The hall light throws my shadow
Down like a grey gauntlet
Squashed and ironed around my feet.
I kick it to one side
As the coat hook beckons for the coat,
Empty and unsatisfied.

## Those Crutches

I take your elbow crutches
To put in the back seat
But they catch on things
Like a pair of coathangers.
I hold them in one hand, giant chopsticks
I could pick up the dog with.
They splay out and resist passively,
As though I'm trying to arrest them.
Finally I use both hands and they behave
And I wonder what your trick is.
Using them must be a stunt
Like not falling off a pair of stilts.

We sit equal in our wheelchair,
All metal and motorised, and no one sees
The pair of sticks stowed in back –
Those ski poles to use without the skis.

# A Small Mortality

There is a small
Hamster-sized void in the house.
There is not much you can say
About a dead hamster.
Never mind the whiskers,
Never mind the cocked ears.
It lived, so it died.
It froze in a dangle-pawed shape
Too sprawling to be alive.
He was very small,
And he must make room
For other hamsters.
But a small mortality
Is no less mortal for being small.
He froze in a form
Familiar but wrong
As I will one day,
Small and needing
To make room for others.

# Old Kent Road

The traffic goes in stripes
Like a long striated muscle
Contracting at the lights.

Gangster traffic demanding
Its own way, cross it
Or double cross at your risk.

Only a clip of documentary
On their wrap-around
Television screens.

I step tentatively on a zebra
Then ride it bareback
Through the Red-Sea gap
When the cars miraculously stop.

Downriver a woman tests
The traffic by pushing
A seated child before her,
A little bullrushed Moses.

# Overnight Express Service

The seats on the coach
Welcome us with open arms
To sit on their laps.

At night lit-up ghost buses
Shadow us, right and left,
Passenger cars sliding under us
In some other dimension.

While we doze like fowls
Gone to roost in the dark,
Our driver, awake on our behalf,
Gouges out our path
With his cowcatcher of light,
Carrying a cargo of sleep
All the way to Thursday morning.

## Flumen Temporis

What gravity at the end of time
Moves the present
Like a river with a waterfall?

What falls off the edge of what
And where, to make
These present moments change?

What mountain spring of time
Feeds our river,
From what drought-free land?

# Rhonabwy

Lie you dreaming on the hide
Of a yellow ox
Of the time when streams were wide
And life a sunny box
Of coloured scarves and golden rings,
Games of chess beneath the trees;
Of the morning look of things
And other pleasures such as these.
'Where?' says the cuckoo bird,
'Where are coloured scarves and chess?'
'Where' – the recurring word;
'Where' – we seek without success.
In the yellow ox's skin,
That is what the past is in.

## Newspaper Vans

In that hotel across the narrow foreign street
From the offices of the *Diário de Notícias*
She died, and all the time she tried to breathe
And we comforted each other
Delivery vans were loading morning papers.

I opened the window to give her air
Her frothy lungs could not hold
And the busy noise rose up those pre-dawn cliffs.

The biggest news on earth
Is that my mother is about to die,
But it doesn't figure in even small headlines
In the *Diário de Notícias* across the street,
Where the vans clatter like dustbin morning.

She lies on the bed trying to breathe
(Beside her the telephone I use,
Controlling my voice
Because I am saying lines in a play, surely),
And the shivaree
At the bottom of the ravine sees her out.
Does she notice the noise
Or only worry at the air,
Wanting to breathe it, noise and all?

In another half hour I am running
Through the lobby
With the ambulance crew;
The street is hotel quiet
Until our useless siren starts.
The paper vans have left;
The news is on its way to foreign breakfasts,
Except the real news.

# Casualty Unit, São José

I sprint after them; I surprise myself;
All the adrenalin has gone to my legs,
I would race them anywhere –
Them and their stretcher.
The young houseman on the graveyard watch
Glances me the truth, but
He proffers a carotid his thick coin
To bribe life back –
Nothing, even magnified.
He relaxes the earphones
To a trick necklace,
Not even bothering to shrug.
The nurse pulls up the blanket
Like someone switching off the picture
Before the story's over.
Indignant, I tug it down again,
Pettily bold, death my ally in defiance.

# Any Hourglass Holds Just So Much Sand

I have seen my future in her whitened hand;
My warm blood will cool, as hers has now.
(Any hourglass holds just so much sand.)

Unexpected scissors snip the magic band –
The woodsman's axe splits off the crucial bough –
I have seen my future in her whitened hand.

We trespass on a borrowed land,
Leave obscure paths through forest, bog and slough.
(Any hourglass holds just so much sand.)

My moving, muscled arm is live and tanned,
But life, it lasts a moment – I think how
I have seen my future in her whitened hand.

A tree once felled can never after stand;
Every living thing at last must bow.
(Any hourglass holds just so much sand.)

Death marks its property with its pale brand,
The waxen page stretched smooth across the brow.
I have seen my future in her whitened hand.
(Any hourglass holds just so much sand.)

# January in Plainfield

Our old wind crosses the tame border,
The only immigrant we never stop to question.
All the years I haven't felt it through my coat
It has still whistled little taunts under Indiana doors.
Now I meet this wind again with crepe on its hat.
When she was alive
Only last week this snow was falling,
Live snow, grey strands in a white-haired sky.
Now it lies in rigid lumps, a growth on the sidewalk.
She is a memory in a thousand minds,
And, careful, I look both ways, proceed with caution,
To protect the fragile part of her that has to last my life.

# DOWN WHERE THE WILLOW
# IS WASHING HER HAIR

## Foreign Expert

I'm an expert – it's written in the contract -
And classes sit at my feet four days a week.
Outside the classroom I revert to ignorance.
The lady selling roasted melon seeds
Has to hold up fingers for the price.
Even the obvious abacus is no good,
Although all over town everyone plays
That rectilinear rosary,
Noisy as ping pong
On all the city's counter-tops.

Banners shout across the street
Messages to everyone but me.

# Down Where the Willow Is Washing Her Hair

Down where the willow is washing her hair
The little arched bridge jumps over the water.
Bikes loaded with melons donkey-like climb
The back of the bridge then run
Down to the lane beside the canal where clothes
Are hung out, clothes and bedclothes
Clean in the sunlight that sifts through the leaves.

Down where the willow is washing her hair
A flatboat glides under the bridge.
A woman cooks fish over coal on the boat
And calls to the man to steer clear of the steps
Where someone is rinsing her rice in the water,
Squatting and swishing a pan at the edge
Of the greenish canal in the shade of the willow.

Down where the willow is washing her hair
A man is selling rush mats.
He made them himself and brought them to town
At dawn on his bike. He charges whatever
The buyer will pay. The mats make beds cooler
In the heat of July, and the man has made more
For tomorrow if he sells what he's brought for today.

Down where the willow is washing her hair
A fight is about to break out.
The crabs from Lake Tai do not weigh anything like
What the seller alleges; the buyer is livid;
Harsh words are exchanged; a crowd forms around them.
Street entertainment is the life of Suzhou;
Performers one day are observers the next.

Down where the willow is washing her hair
A corner of town lives its various lives.
A girl tries out a new hair-do and dreams
Of a boy she hasn't yet met. Is it he
On the bike with a new video camera strapped
On the back? What a dash he is cutting as he rides
Past where the willow is washing her hair!

# Suzhou Students Playing Tennis

The tennis courts are unrolled clay
But the students persevere and play
In spite of having not one net.
Tennis! Well, how bourgeois can you get?
Were they thrown out by the proles,
Seeing they were full of holes?
The students excel at make-do-and-mending,
At lateral thinking and blatant rule-bending.
They play unselfconsciously in front of me
With a row of bikes where the net should be.

# Miss Zhou Drops a Bombshell

'You may not believe this,' she says,
Challenging me to imagine –
Pausing to let me prepare myself –
'But
Not everyone
In China
Has
A television set.'
The bathos leaves me speechless
But she reads it
As shock at deprivation.

# Three Time Pieces

## I. THE CLOCK BUILDING

Left behind like an old hymnal
By the Methodists who set the place ticking,
The Clock Building is neo-everything in brick.
Toward the end of term I take
My older class around the walls
And tell them why the chapel window
Looks like that. 'This is Gothic,' I say,
And 'That looks French.'

But the neglect is pure Chinese.
The clock is stopped in four directions
Like a dried-up lighthouse in a sea of trees.
Ten-to-three splays across the face,
Behind which lies a cube of empty space.

## II. MY WRISTWATCH LYING ON THE LECTERN

I slip it off my wrist as the bell's ringing
And lay it within glancing range.
This quartz sand runs through the class,
Startling me variously by its speed.
It's right to the second, as the bells,
I notice, certainly aren't.
I set it by the BBC
Every now and then, GMT.

They know the class is over
When I fit it back on my pale bracelet
As I describe their hurdle for next week.
They're impatient, but I make them wait;
The bell goes, a minute and many seconds late.

### III. ALARM CLOCK

A good alarm, but overeager.
Every night I have to rein it in
When I'm giving it instructions
For the morning.
         But at six I wake
And watch that restless hand edge
Toward smaller angles. I am Faustus,
Monday morning my midnight.
Oh, *currite lente*! Hold off a little while.
Why this relentless gallop down the dial?

# Eastern China Air, Flight to Beijing

Shanghai is falling out of the bottom of the plane
As we swivel north over the Yangtze delta,
But then the clouds discreetly cover up
Anything we shouldn't see.
The clouds are working for the Party
And they're among the higher-ups.

The clouds nearer Beijing
Have an Open Policy, and far below
The fields lie like floorboards,
Long and flat on the land,
Keeping secrets in the cellar.

## Drinking Game

Miss Wang likes a beer as much
As any student in the West.
We play an old Chinese drinking game.
She shows me how it works:
Stone breaks scissors, she explains,
But how China, why drinking?
I catch on fast. She must think
I'm apt, a genius.
                    We sit at the party
In our coats, as it's December
Indoors and out, but for a moment
I recall Sunday best and sermons
More for grown-ups. Not drinking then,
But winning bouts with boredom,
Our clandestine gestures between us on the pew,
Passing God's time.
                    My student Wang,
Glad but foxed, gets to drink a lot of beer
As I keep winning bouts.
For a beginner I do all right
But it's a game of chance, after all,
And when her paper wraps my rock
I have a consolation swig of pale Dong Wu.
The only drink in church was communion wine
That wasn't wine. Miss Wang, what memories of mine
Would make any sense to you?

# In Yangshuo for Semester Break

The Li River has carved caves
Dripping with uvulae,
As the English language,
Getting to my mouth first,
Has eroded it into its own shape.

We are professional breaths of fresh air here,
But now we are off duty.
Braziers smoulder under the table
At the Green Lotus Wine Shop
As we plan a saunter through the market.
At night we go to watch
The fisherman's cormorants diving
And delivering river fish to his funnel net.

We are oil in a land of water,
Floating on the Li River
And floating on China.

Back in the Green Lotus Wine Shop,
Where Mo has muesli on the menu,
We are talking to some new-made friends.
Caroline from Melbourne says she's seen
A brand-new Chinese washing machine
That plays 'Joy to the World' when the cycle ends.

# Beowulf *in China*

We're finishing *Beowulf* today
Too fast, in simple modern English,
Summarised and shortened in their home-grown text,
But I try to compensate;
I make the story as exciting as I can.
Here are the spear-Danes in yore-days,
Here is Beowulf the Geat, the fighting man.

It's all new to them: it's hard to keep things straight
When the textbook's flawed and they don't catch all I say.
I explain the Anglo-Saxon view of fate
And the atmosphere the scenes convey.
Later on the final they get it, in the main,
But he is 'Prince of Denmark', that other English Dane.

I have my vision of Hrothgar's home,
The drinking hall of the ring-giver,
The rough, Germanic, hero hall,
But even now I know
That along the swan-path of my words,
My meaning drowns in Chinese lecture notes.
My students are giving Beowulf a mandarin moustache;
Scrolls of calligraphy grace the walls
Of Heorot, the mead pavilion
Where Hrothgar's courtiers died.
Golden carp glitter darkly in the pool
Where Grendel and his dam reside.

Beowulf meets Grendel in an empty-handed midnight bout
And karates off an arm as Hrothgar's warriors watch
(Or 'worriers' on the final,
But Grendel had them worried, did he not?)

I cannot stop this Chinesing of the Anglo-Saxon tale.
It's happening with every word I say.
I can hear all my explanations fail;
Differing assumptions keep getting in the way.
Beowulf, Hrothgar, Grendel – the whole gang –
Are becoming figures of the Early Tang.

# Doing Donne

(Suzhou University, Spring semester)

I know these are umbrellas, but for today
They are a compass, or pair of compasses,
As Donne says. Dee how I hold them at the top:
When one leg moves, the other leans the same
Direction. Donne is one leg, the lady is the other.
'Conceit' we call this; Donne the master poet
Used these metaphors, extended to
The breaking point, 'like gold to airy thin-
Ness beat'.
           The umbrellas – compasses, I mean –
Are joined, even though the bottom ends
Are far apart.  So the poet's soul
Is one with the lady's soul – joined
You see, in spite of all appearances.

And I am running this far perimeter
Myself, still joined by letters and the odd
Phone call. I've better postal service than
John Donne, but then I've travelled farther than
He could have done. When I have done, then I
Will leave my Donne behind, as that is what
Is done by foreign teachers here, the done
Thing, as Jack himself would say.

Remember this example of conceit,
A metaphysical conceit. It may
Well be a question on the midterm test.

# Merry Christmas, Surely

Our mentors spent half the joyful day
Stringing coloured lights under the bam,
Under the boo, under the bam
Boo and camphor trees.
Floods of fairy lights gush off my balcony.
They know Christmas is in December
And English speakers will demand
The props of myth, deliciously novel here.
It's to do with pine trees and a gnome in red
As politically correct as you could wish;
They know for sure we send cards,
Hang tinsel from the ceiling
And revel in certain songs;
They have all the evidence.

We are stuck with their secondhand surmise.
In vain we demur, explain the extenuations
Of agnosticism, of Chanukkah,
Of simple diversity. 'Commercialism,' we begin,
Realising just too late it's their ideal.
We go through the motions for them,
Going through the motions for us.
Finally in March two of us nod without a word,
Get up on chairs after lunch
And unpin the tinsel swags.

# The Foreign Expert Discourses on Irony

I am teaching irony ('Why
Does Mr Bennet say this to his daughter?')
And today I wear it, too.
This jacket from my mother's things
Wasn't on the scene in time to stand
In front of any of the many classes
She retired from, but there's no escape,
And now the sleeves have made their teacher-gestures anyway.

She couldn't have imagined the fine snowfall
Of daily Chinese chalk drifting on the cuffs.
I write 'irony' on the board
And think a wink at my arm.

## Lunch at the Bamboo Grove

(for Carol Strawn)

When we needed a break
From the noise and dirt and incomprehension
We met for lunch at the Bamboo Grove Hotel.
They tucked you into your napkin
And poured your coffee for you,
All with an obsequious flourish
They thought we needed.
The hotel was a time-out spot
In the game called China
Where we nibbled a hole in the afternoon.
Lunch was comparing college days
And reverting to our Midwest talk;
Lunch was having another pot of coffee
(No, honestly, we'll pour it ourselves)
And a chocolate thing the Singapore chef
Picked up in Paris.
           The waitresses –
Three times as many as they needed –
Stared at the strangers
Who took refuge in that patch of not-China
Waving off their trained servility
And chortling over things that would have taken
Hours of explanation.
           But we refreshed each other
For another week of China,
Swinging toward the end of our stint
From Friday to Friday like gymnasts.

# Final Exam in the Green Building

Lu and I are patrolling our English students;
He set half the exam and I the other,
And now we're harvesting the semester,
Meeting here among our students
Like reapers seeing how the seeds have grown.
Now we move in opposition around the room;
We are doubles partners covering the court,
Our vision acute in angles.

Our scribblers crouch, perched on flat-out elbows
Among their debris of test-taking:
Extra pens, a watch, a glasses case.
But what are they making of it all?
Under all that thick black hair
How are they dealing with Adam and the Fall?
What are they doing with Jane Austen and Jane Eyre?

# A Byronic Valediction to Suzhou University

The end of the semester's drawing near –
I can hardly wait for it to end!
I have spent quite long enough round here.
Today I got my trunk all packed to send,
Full of tapes and books and other gear,
Winter clothes and gifts for every friend.
And now I'm counting days until it's time
To go and writing up this little rhyme.

You see, I've spent the last week teaching Keats
And other poets of the day, like Byron,
That tireless teller of his own fine feats
Whose constitution surely was of iron.
He wrote *sin fin* about Don Juan's beats,
A subject that he never seemed to tire on.
Ottava rima holds the bouncy chatter –
At length you catch the rhythm of the patter.

So roll on, roll on, the end of year!
I'm keen to leave, but yet I look around
And feel a pang of something like mild fear
Of failing to recall some sight or sound –
The way osmanthus hovers in the air
Or yellow gingko leaves drift on the ground.
What will I remember, what forget?
How fine will be the mesh that makes my net?

## Day-Bags

By ten o'clock the day is a long canvas bag
Stuffed bulging with lumpy hours,
Filled out and hard.
I pull weary strings to close this bag,
Pushing it, kicking it, to its place
In the corner with all the others.
Bright yellow, it fades to grey by morning
When I wake and find a yellow draw-string bag
Folded neatly on the foot of my bed.

## Measuring the Net

The last time I measured a net like this
Was more than twenty years ago
On a hot dry court in an Indiana town
Where everybody played – I always explain
It was nothing special, nothing expensive.
We were taught to measure the net
With the height and width of the racket
Making thirty-six inches. We wanted to do it right;

We shook hands at the end and we always wore white.
In doubles Jackie and I pooled our backhands,
Foxing opponents who expected one of each.
Hot summers of our teens till the shadows oozed
Across those slow clay courts we strode and wheeled,
Sending back any ball inside our baselines.
By the end of June our burns had peeled,

Calluses formed and blisters healed.
Now I begin to play again at odd times
In hours doled out by the court-keeper
When my few tennis-playing friends are free.
On a cool London evening after rain
I take my oldest racket with the nylon strings
In case the court is damp. My serve
Is as tarnished as a teapot ageing in an attic.
Am I playing at my adolescence,
Calling up a younger self
Who spent her summers on the hard-packed clay?
Perhaps even singles is still doubles
As the white-clad girl just out of sight beside me
Rushes up behind a backhand drive,
Still sixteen, the one who spent the spring
Idly doodling tennis courts, the floodlights and the fence
Instead of conjugating the pluperfect tense.

## Letter to Christine de Pisan (1365-1431?) Written During a Pause in Translating Her Into English

Christine, Christine!
What did you mean?
What is this word
I've never heard
Before? And why
Oh why can't I
Find it, tiny
Shard of shiny
Verb in the book
Where I look?
Middle French
On the turn,
What a wrench
To try to learn
Your French, Christine!
Oh, what *did* you mean?
Wish I knew
Whether you
Had meant to say
It just this way;
Wish that you
Could send a few
Words to me
Just to see,
Smuggled out
Of the stout redoubt
Of the Count of Time
To say that I'm
Doing OK.
What do you say?

## We Are a Committee of Two

We are a committee of two
Formed to deal
With your concerns, my concerns.
Take some misfortune, say:
One of us is a plaintiff
And the other a kind of samurai,
Outraged and waving weapons,
Furious as a train with failing brakes.
So misfortunes,
What we used to call misfortunes,
Are little shrinking things
Whispering, I didn't mean it, honest.

## On the Beach

On the beach all the shells
Hoard up tales of waves
To confide to the first
Human ear that wants to know.
We scuff over them in boots,
Ignoring the high fidelity gossip
Underfoot, intent on our own sound swapping.
Not quite agreeing, we define and trade,
Refine, accept, insist, sinking our thick treads
Rhythmically into the shifting shingle,
Carelessing bits of bivalve and fisted shells
Bursting to tell us all they've learned.

## Notes in Advance

I shall remind you of my death
Now when it seems far away.
I shall describe it
And what you will feel
And what you must avoid.
By saying all this now
Do I outwit the final silence?
Standing by my coffin,
You will know that
I've already shared this with you,
That I would comfort you now
But for this inconvenience.
I have done it in advance
As, going abroad in April,
We write notes in March
For the summer guests.

# My Father on Monument Circle

My father is a rumour who has reached
My ears, a little list of attributes
Who played clarinet and tennis,
Won a prize in Tort,
And in the afterglow of Lindbergh
Went aloft in jodhpurs.
One warm day in 1935
Somebody snapped me a rare souvenir,
Stopped him in mid-stride
In a linen suit, developed him into an image
Before I had one. My father strides stylishly
In a wide pale hat, still in his twenties
Where it is always a summer before the war.
Later he tossed me half a baton
And then lost interest in the race.
I watch him now when he never guessed
I might be looking, thanks to the man
Who did me a favour for a dime one pastel summer.

## Collecting Material

Let me through!
Let me through!
I'm collecting
material for an
autobiography!
I must see
everything
even if
it only goes
in a footnote.
Don't crowd in
a ring around
something I can use.
Don't say
come back later
don't bother us
we're busy
we'll let you know
come back when
we've got it cleaned up.
I've got to
collect my material.

## Twiddling the Wheel

Tomorrow might be several things
Or several other things.
Even the next hour has not happened yet.
We are always forming hours,
Like a potter never away from his wheel.
Say we carry a shaping wheel everywhere
Always with us, always twiddling it,
Pedalling at it, running wet fingers
Around the inside of slick hours.

## Boy Diving

The diving board, hempen covered,
Bounces the confident
Into twelve clear feet of water.
The boy walks his plank, shivers,
Knows the older boys watch.
The rope beneath his feet
Licks like a lion's tongue;
At the end the water pauses
And waits with its mouth open.
He pictures in the air the shape he makes,
Then hides under the blue disturbance
To rise later, unconcerned, somebody else.

## Despite Persistent Ill-Health

'In the 1920s, despite persistent ill-health, he had considerable success with nudes...' (note on Mark Gertler at Royal Academy exhibition)


Here, here,
My dear,
You're half awake.
Let's take a break.
Shall we sit
For a bit
On the bed?
I've caught your head –
Your hair, that blush –
With my brush.
I love this line,
My dear, so fine,
So fine, and this –
Just let me kiss
Your rounded arm
(Where's the harm?)
Let's slip this off
(Damn this cough!)

# The Man Has Come to Tune the Typewriter

The man has come to tune the typewriter;
He is upset because C is not in the middle.
It is not my fault,
I have told him,
But he says it is my typewriter
And I am responsible.
I am responsible
For C not being in the middle.
His logic is flawless,
He tells me.
I suppose I am responsible,
Because his logic is flawless.
I shall keep C where it is
Because I'm used to it there,
But I have agreed to feel guilty.

# My Life Is a Long Striped Cat

My life is a long striped cat
Feeling her way through the tall grass.
There are hornet nests and water,
Obstacles and twining plants.

My life is a twining plant
Feeling its way past hornet nests and water,
Climbing above the long, low cat,
Rising through and above the tall grass.

My life is a field of tall grass
Containing hornet nests and water
Where a wandering hidden cat
Creeps among the twining plants.

## Pierson's Boyhood

Old Pierson lived until his life
Slid out from under him and he was left
Explaining himself to children.
Not generous, he read the paper
And did arithmetic in private.
Finally the oldest man that Pierson knew
Had met him when Pierson was eighteen,
And Pierson's boyhood could not be vouched for
By any living soul.
This alone Pierson would have shared,
Would have paid a man to remember.

## The Tightrope Walker

He balances on the tenuous trust of the rope
And carries his consciousness in his feet,
Sliding them one in front of the other.
We watch as though we are all roped together
With him, the guide of the expedition.
He has been here before, guiding others.
We trust him not to fall, not to falter,
Not to do anything we fear he might.
He may be up there trusting us
To trust him, or trusting us
To have doubts, and all the time
He walks his cat's walk overhead,
Feeling the rope with his toes
And making a groove in his foot.
When we all arrive at the far platform
We will take off our goggles
And shake hands all around,
Glad to reach the camp and take off
The ropes, even though we trusted them.

## Visit to a Cottage

With eyes that never need a magnifying glass
You examine window sills and lintels
Of this ordinary cottage
Half hidden from the traffic by some trees.
I stand beside you in your old boots
Wondering how my week-end afternoons
Have turned so windy and mud footed.
Now like a horse dealer reading teeth
You finger over these roofless bricks,
And I, untrained in weathered brickwork, look at you.
I shall not write a monograph of findings;
I make no notes for lectures to the public.
I will keep this to myself;
How, scuffing these wellingtons that you wore,
Slightly apart I watch and stand
As you touch a mouldered window, crazy door,
With your careful, uncommitted, ringless hand.

# Thirteen Ways of Looking at a Ball of Old String

(for Glen Lee)


I.

A ball of old string
Is a way of carrying
Fifteen yards in your pocket.


II.

A ball of old string
Is a hundred knots
That might be tied.


III.

The kite thinks
It could be a bird
Roosting at night in the clouds
If not for that ball of old string.

IV.

A ball of old string
Is a child's plaything,
An adult's saving against stringlessness.

V.

Inside a golf ball
A thousand rubber bands
Pretend to be a ball of old string.

VI.

A ball of old string
Grows bigger,
Layered like tree rings.

VII.

Where is the ball of old string
When you need it?

VIII.

You say wonderingly
I could find something interesting
In a ball of old string,
And, dear friend,
I believe you're right.


IX.

A ball of old string
Can even roll into
The corners of a poem.


X.

A ball of old string
Has something in common with a blackbird;
Thirteen balls of string
Share something with thirteen blackbirds.


XI.

I had not thought of this ball of old string
Until you mentioned it,
And see how it has unwound in my mind.

XII.

Several balls of old string
Can become one ball of old string,
And one ball contains many.


XIII.

A ball of old string
Is what you make of it.

## At the Sheepdog Trials

Don't know why they watch
Dog so much. It's us
Does it. We know
The gates, the turns,
All he does, he follows behind
Maybe to one side, big deal,
So what, and people come
From over the hills to look.
Maybe they like the way we move
All together. Takes a little practice
And have to break dog in.

Like to get round behind
Dog for once, don't like him
Always in corner of eye
Looking shifty. Don't think
He bites. May bite.
Don't see how dog
Does it, just one of him
And nowt to lead.

Here he comes
In his straight black wool.
Heel!
There, it worked. Doesn't
Always work.

# The Brass Anvil

My mother's father lived in my first ten years,
But stayed behind as I grew older.

To stretch my memories out where I can touch them
I have a frost-heaved arrowhead
Found one April behind his plough,
Photographs that chart the whitening of his hair,
And now a two-inch-long brass anvil
From a London market stall this morning.
My little golden talisman
Dazzles my mind back to the anvil he had,
Left over from the forge in his arrowheaded days.

All the way home from the market
I hefted it in my hand
And thought of the way he used to peel an apple,
Just for the fun of doing it,
In one long linen-lined red curl.

## Souvenir of Stornoway

In Stornoway I bought the language,
Green-bound in a bookshop.

This is a telescope for seeing another world
Lived in without a second thought
As I live in my world
Where nothing happens without English verbs.

In this green language
The word for 'green' is the word for 'blue',
One word for 'blue' is a word for 'grey',
And *glas*, meaning 'grey', is another word for 'green'.
They have ten different words for 'mountain'.

That world a telescope away from English
Where certain shades of green are blue
Sits on my shelf; I possess on loan
Perfect bound ten different kinds of mountain.

## Below the Surface

I.

The passage of time is written
All over us, individual the way our handwriting
Differed on notes in study hall.
Their children are older than we were then.

Our old yearbook pictures
Have aged into other people.
In our memories the others support or star –
Now it hardly matters which.
We are a club with impromptu meetings
And time is the only dues.

II.

Home towns stay there idling quietly
Without you. Danville exists
On the map and in my memory,
None too compatibly.

They retired the old road
And trained up a new one
Twice the size to take its place.
It sneaks into town
Behind the County Home,
An old landmark mirror-imaged.

I came here for that chill afternoon
Last week when the mortician and I
Paced and pointed like a pair of Andrew Jacksons
Decreeing the Capitol.
I had carved the name and dates
By airmail. Later he will fix them
Like a paperweight on the earth.

I have discharged the duty Death dumped on me.
Always a practical joker with no taste,
He gave me a foreign canister
To run football-like home to these end-posts.

III.

We admire each other's faces,
The yearbook overlain with years.
We are cousins of a kind,
Joined by things we hold in common.
We were born intimate friends;
We know each other's middle names.

If we pooled our lives we could show
Degrees and diplomas, some tangential deaths,
A dozen children, four or five divorces,
A navy stint, careers and changed careers,
Miscellaneous experience,
And abilities we'd never heard of
In the embryonic then.

We assume answering features
In each other's lives.
Survivors so far of our customised
Obstacle courses, we ex-boys and -girls
Share the secrets of our generation.
We sense unspoken passwords;
The secret handshake is an easy embrace.

IV.

Death, always wanting the last word –
The vulgar little pest leers
With his stopwatch cocked.
He has sent me on a business trip,
But he is not the boss he thinks.
He is a minor item, a pompous bully
With no sense of decency.
I've got his number every bit as much
As he's got mine.

## V.

We could all disinter
Squabbles from junior high.
We share a childish past,
But in the present we admire each other
As Mr Etienne might have approved
Of varying but right solutions in our homework.
We have reached this age ingeniously;
Everyone has done it in ways
Not occurring to the others.
Delight veneers our voices.
A paragraph is in our smiles.
Fancy meeting you here
At this time of life.

VI.

The alphabet threw us together
In Freshman English,
Juggled us differently downstairs in history.
We went to summer camp;
With overlapping others
We wore our best on Sundays.
We wore our wool bermudas
To football games –
Went to watch Bob play
(Bob, now badly bald,
Father of four,
Married a cheerleader, also here).
Through the ravages of gravity
And depredations of the calendar and clock
We recognise ourselves.
We are mirrors having a party,
Two-way mirrors sharing a joke.

## VII.

This afternoon in the older part of town
Houses we used to live in
Gazed back at me.
Their owners won't know what ghosts of mine
Sit on invisible furniture.
The family mansions are now all
The green, low-lintelled kind,
But I see through ancestral eyes.
I know where the tracks used to run
And where the Chautauqua was.
I am inhabitant, historian, descendant
And ghost pacing through my streets.

These spring streets shimmer with the past.
On the courthouse square, the reason for the town,
I see the band concerts on the lawn
In the cool of summer evenings,
Mr Skidmore, a grey bear in uniform,
Gouging out the music with his stick.
It's all still here below the surface,
As indeed they all are, I think,
Who have no family left in town above the grass.

VIII.

Sherry used to teach home-ec,
Is now a lawyer; Janet married medicine
And teaches in the grades;
Now we three braid ourselves again.
Somewhere in the back of a drawer
That's rarely opened there must be
A black and white snap
Of us madly cross-dressed in togas,
A giggling triumvirate in drag,
Purple striped and tickled pink.
*'Sacra bos!'* we exclaimed
With the erudition of the not-yet-educated.
*'Tu me mittis,'*† we sang, quoting Johnny Mathis.
None of this comes out in words tonight,
But still our contogate past
Underlies this present as Mr Skidmore does
The empty courthouse lawn.

* 'Holy Cow!'
† 'You send me'.

IX.

On North Washington my mind skirts
The pile of bricks from the Thompson House,
The whole end wall tornadoed
Into Good Friday afternoon one year.
The town is divided into those who remember
And those who don't.

Weaver ran one funeral home,
Divided the dead with Baker at the other.
Now Weaver's gone south to live,
Leaving his young partner to bury
Their half share.
Enter I, requiring services.
(He's not a local man, I grasp at once.
I, a stranger turning up,
Have the drop on him,
Local-knowledge-wise.)
We discuss the job at hand.
He likes his work, chose it, even.
He handles death like a salesman trading cars,
But he's got steadier work,
A more dependable clientele.

## X.

We are re-enacting parties of our youth,
But now attended entirely by our parents.
We're all drinking Diet Coke,
The *vin de pays* here,
And making jigsaw puzzles of ourselves,
Exclaiming over pieces found.
We share the dilemmas and decisions
Of each other's lives without needing
To know exactly what they are.
We remember when we were
More what met the eye.

We drove our parents' cars,
Knew each other's tail-fins at a glance.
We borrowed the night for a movie in the city;
Weekend nights featured drive-in friends
And the rituals of teams and games.

Glenn's in computers, Norman does research,
Cynthia analyses blood all day.
How we frayed apart from the rope we were!
(Karen brings around some food.
We are at her house, carpeted and lit
In the latest style. We contribute praise
To her select collection.)

When the talk stops for breath
Somebody's pet lightning strikes
To fix us sitting here together
Playing at the former rope.
Later we will exchange
These moments skewered by the light,
A trade of time we all possess.

## XI.

The Reed stone marks the centre
Of the plot like a parent plant
Seeding smaller headstones.
We find a spot between my grandparents –
So she ends where she began.
This looks like a neighbourhood
Condensed from life. They are always
At home here, but never receive.
I am separated by six feet
From the ones I never knew.

Weaver's man's never heard
Of Great-aunt Ada and her shocking
Accidental death, but I think
Seeing her name here
Of the family story
That began in 1934.
Then I turn to agree
About the placement.
'Yes, there,' I say.
'Just there is fine.'

## XII.

I fly with a Buick Skylark
To corners of the county
No public bus has ever touched.
I get re-used to driving on the right
And the power-steering twirl.
'My Skylark,' I call it,
As though it weren't the rental man
Who introduced us.
It rolls me over the roads
I used to take in Fords.

The dashboard clip holds all the notes
Of directions to front doors
I made then (cuddling the phone,
Picturing the route as I wrote it down).
North to this junction, west to that,
Left at the church, bypassing the bypass.
My scrappy social calendar gets haywire
When I turn the knob for music
And a few front doors flutter to the floor.

XIII.

I'm visiting the past, where other people live.
I drop in on thirty years ago,
And watch it through a one-way glass.

I gee-up the Skylark back to rent-a-bird,
Waved off by the shade of Mr Skidmore
On the courthouse lawn and bumping over
The non-existent interurban tracks.

Good-bye again, but not for good;
I'm taking part of the town away.

The County Home, islanded between
Past and now, stands left
Instead of right as I pass where
The town limits used to be.
The rear-view mirror watches the town grow small;
The rear-view mirror sees the past recede.